T0194289

I Married My Judas

A Divine Revelation

E. JAROSLAWA

WESTBOW
PRESS®
A DIVISION OF THOMAS NELSON
& ZONDERVAN

WestBow Press books may be ordered through booksellers or by contacting:

WestBow Press
A Division of Thomas Nelson & Zondervan
1663 Liberty Drive
Bloomington, IN 47403
www.westbowpress.com
1 (866) 928-1240

ISBN: 978-1-9736-5136-9 (sc)
ISBN: 978-1-9736-5135-2 (e)

Print information available on the last page.

WestBow Press rev. date: 03/19/2019

I Married My Judas is dedicated with love to my family. I thank my parents for their strength, honesty, and commitment every day as they taught me how to live, love, and treasure family.

I thank my daughter for teaching me how to set my priorities and live by my expected standards without compromising.

I thank my sisters for believing and trusting in me.

I thank my brothers for always protecting me.

I thank my nephew for giving me sight during my darkness.

And I thank the love of my life for always loving me, especially during the dark moments.

From then on he began looking for a
good opportunity to betray Jesus.
—Matthew 26:16 (KJV)

Foreword

When looking back at the very familiar story of Judas and his horrendous betrayal of Christ, it is no doubt that in most minds, Judas was the greatest sinner of all time. How could someone betray another unto death, who has trusted, nurtured, taught, and most importantly loved you?

Judas was chosen to be an apostle by Jesus. He spent three and a half years traveling and learning of Christ. He watched miracle after miracle that Christ performed, proclaimed his love for him, but still betrayed him.

Just as Judas betrayed his Lord and friend, the very same thing happens to most of us. We give so much of ourselves to others only to find out that it was all in vain. We spend so much time loving, nurturing, caring, and encouraging people who really don't have our best interest at heart, leaving us feeling hurt, abused, misused, and taken advantage of.

Jesus, in his omniscient splendor, knew Judas was going to betray him, but he still embraced him. We must learn to embrace the Judases in our lives. Stand strong and allow Judas's works push you into your destiny. Judas's betrayal allowed Jesus to fulfill the will and the work of the Father.

So instead of turning away from or dismissing your Judases, embrace the moment. No matter if it's a loved one, friend, or enemy, it will ultimately push you into your destiny.

Chapter 1
The Beginning

On August 24, 1989, I married my Judas. My name is Tia Summers and my ex-husband's name is Samuel Summers. We have a daughter named Jai Summers, who is now seventeen. Our love for our daughter pushed our marriage as far as it could go. Even though the marriage was stormy from the very beginning, it lasted for twenty-seven years. We were both young and immature at the time the marriage took place. Throughout the marriage, there was laughter, pain, growth, and hardship. We both learned valuable lessons as we experienced life together during our shared innocence.

Some of the best memories took place within the early months of our marriage. I remember we were so broke; we had very little food and money. I was working part time, and Samuel became unemployed a few days after we were married. Still, we ate well every day because he was a great fisherman, who loved to fish. He would fish almost every day to bring home our meal. Therefore, we ate fish and potatoes almost daily. We did not mind, for we both loved fish, so we learned to cook it a variety of ways. Looking back, our broke days were our better days spent together. We learned to trust and depend on each other. We had only one vehicle for transportation, so we were together more than apart. Our only means of transportation was a car with just an AM radio station. Because our preferred music choice was unavailable, we usually talked during the entire drive anywhere, so we learned how to communicate and connect well with each other. We had one television in our home, so we accommodated each other more. Although these conditions may seem to have been unfavorable, they allowed us to get to know each other better. Over the years, we became intertwined.

Nevertheless, years later, we both became irritable and uncaring toward each other, so we felt ending the marriage was best. It soon became evident that the marriage was intolerable. The divorce was finalized on July 24, 2016. Two weeks later, Samuel remarried.

E. Jaroslawa

Chapter 2

The Morning of the Betrayal, Part 1

It was 4:00 a.m., and I was awakened by the sound of the front door repeatedly opening and closing. I quietly tiptoed to the door to find my husband standing there with a surprised look on his face as he was carrying bags to his car. I asked him, "What are you doing?"

He replied, "I am leaving you, and I am taking our daughter with me!"

I replied, "You can leave, but our daughter stays."

I became hysterical; I cried, yelled, and screamed. I ran back into the house and looked in my daughter's bedroom. She was there, still sleeping. I felt relieved.

Just as I went to lock the front door, he threw

papers at me. The papers fell inside the house as I closed the door. I began to read them—they were a notification that he was asking for a divorce and sole custody of Jai. I became very upset. I cried, screamed, and yelled even more.

What is happening? I began to ask myself. I felt my life turning upside down. I felt I had lost control of being a wife and mother. How could this be happening? Why was this happening? How could I make this nightmare go away? My mind was racing at a high speed; I couldn't catch up with the many thoughts or questions, much less process anything that entered my mind. So I sat down at my dining room table and began to calm myself down. I prayed and meditated. Oddly, I received a sense of calmness centered around the madness that surrounded me, and from that very moment I felt God's presence and knew I was not alone. Deep down in the pit of my stomach, I felt my nerves reveal to me that somehow everything would turn around and work out for the good that was meant to be.

Chapter 3
The Morning of the Betrayal, Part 2

Later, I went back to bed and fell asleep. I woke up at the sound of my alarm clock. It was now 6:30 a.m. and time to get my thirteen-year-old daughter, Jai, up for school. Ordinarily, I stood at the front door as my daughter waited at the end of the driveway until the bus arrived at 7:20 a.m. However, this morning was no ordinary morning. It had been a morning of chaos and disruption. Once the bus left, I began seeking legal advice for the matters at hand.

The bus left at 7:23 a.m. I closed the door and began the task of making phone calls and leaving messages in hopes of receiving returned calls. With every call, I began listening to advice and taking notes for my own knowledge and insight.

After the calls, I showered, got dressed, and headed out the door for my busy day's journey.

My first stop was to the ATM to check on the balance of one of the joint accounts I shared with my husband. The balance was $2.08. I laughed and thought to myself, *Well, at least the account has a positive balance rather than negative.* I became upset again.

The next stop was to a nearby law office. I knew I had to humble myself before I appeared in this prominent African American law firm. This law firm was owned and operated by a practicing husband and wife team, both of whom were well-respected individuals in this historic, rural county. They are well-known and loved by many. Mrs. Blackwell is a retired judge and had previously worked as the commonwealth attorney for many years. Her husband is presently a judge.

As I walked into the office, I was greeted by an employee who appeared professional and caring. He informed me that Mrs. Blackwell would see me in a few minutes as she finished up with a client who was in her office. I waited. Mrs. Blackwell finished and came out to the waiting area. She greeted me and asked me to come into her office.

As I followed her, she immediately asked me, "How can I help you today, Mrs. Summers?"

I replied, "I need help in dealing with these documents." I informed her that I had received the documents from my husband earlier that morning when I found him sneaking around, taking bags of his belongings to his car. I handed her the packet, and she began to read as she listened to me give her details of my early morning events. She asked why the documents had not been served by the proper authority as they would in normal proceedings. I replied, "I do not know." She asked how long Mr. Summers and I had been separated. I replied, "He just left home this morning."

Mrs. Blackwell explained the documents to me. She attempted to contact my husband's listed attorney, there was no answer. She began typing a letter and continued explaining the documents. She informed me that my husband and his attorney appeared to be trying to use the tactic of petitioning for a divorce under false pretenses. She pointed out important factors on the documents that suggested Mr. Summers and I had been separated for several months now. Next, the document detailed that I had relocated and abandoned my family and I was living at a new address. And lastly, it stated that my husband was seeking alimony, child support, and full custody of my daughter.

Chapter 4
The Revelation

Each time I read over the papers, I began to understand in greater detail. So, naturally, I became even more frustrated and tearful. How could someone who proclaimed to love me betray me in such a manner, hiding such dark secrets? How could he only care about his own personal gain? It was unbeknownst to me. I realized at that very moment that I had been married to someone for over twenty years and yet I did not know him. I immediately thought to myself, *I married my Judas!*

How could this be? I loved this man! I trusted him! I slept with him! I took care of him! We had a daughter together! We were a family! How could I have been so stupid for allowing this to happen? What would my family, friends, and other people say when they found out about this mess? I was in shock and disbelief all at once. I became speechless, as if my tongue had been ripped from my mouth.

This was much bigger than I could have ever imagined. My life would no longer be the same in many ways. Everything I had come to know over the last twenty-five years was a lie. I did not know my husband, and in many ways, I no longer knew myself. But I refused to be the victim in this fight. I was in this situation because I was naïve and had not discerned my husband's evil intent. Regardless, I planned to fight back. I decided to go about this with clean hands, using the legal system. My plan of action would be to do things properly and with order for better results. First, I would need to empower myself with knowledge about the legal system concerning a battle of this nature. Then I would need to remain focused and determined to follow through until the end.

At the end of our appointment, Mrs. Blackwell had prepared and given me the letter as well as legal advice. We agreed to stay in contact. As I was leaving her office, she assured me all things would work out fine. I believed her for the most part, even though I had many doubts about possible unfavorable outcomes while living in this small rural community where everyone was seemingly connected to somebody. This made laws seem watered down. If a person knows the right person, there is a greater chance of a lesser punishment awarded for wrongdoing in this community.

E. Jaroslawa

Chapter 5
The Evening of the Betrayal

I headed back home to get things in order before Jai arrived home from school. At 3:36 p.m., I noticed the bus had passed by my home without making a stop for my daughter. I called her cell phone, but the call went immediately to voicemail. I called the school, and the school secretary informed me that Mr. Summers had taken our daughter out of school early. I called my husband, and the call went immediately to voicemail. I began to panic. I paced back and forth throughout my home and made phone calls to friends and family to see if anyone had seen or knew of my daughter's whereabouts. Hours later, my husband pulled up in the driveway with my daughter. He asked if we could sit quietly and talk about our situation. He wanted to talk about our failing marriage.

We talked while our daughter went into her bedroom. He apologized and asked if he could come back home and start over. I told him I didn't trust him or his judgment anymore. He reassured me he would change. So I agreed. I only agreed because I feared having my daughter stolen from me. Everything within me told me not to trust him. I knew he was not being sincere, but at least I would have my daughter back home where she belonged.

As the evening went on, we both pretended everything was normal. We each went our separate ways in the house as usual. He went into the living room where he laid on the sofa watching television, I went into my bedroom to watch television, and Jai was in her room.

Six months went by and everything remained the same. We talked, laughed, and went places as usual. But every day I felt an uneasy feeling about our lives—it was too peaceful. I knew a great change was about to take place. I worked a lot of overtime on my two jobs and later picked up a third job for extra cash to pay bills. Even though my husband had just started a new job four weeks ago, he still refused to help pay bills, claiming he was not making enough money and that he had to repay people who lent him money during his two years of unemployment. Of course, I did not believe him. I knew he was stashing money away for his next move.

E. Jaroslawa

Chapter 6

The Lies

Monday evening after Mother's Day, I was off work. I decided to do some cleaning and other chores around the house. Later that evening when Jai came home from school, I decided to iron clothes while watching television in the den with her. In between commercial breaks, we would have small talks, so Jai began to tell me how she spent Mother's Day with her dad while I was at work. I asked her about the church service on Sunday. She told me she and her dad did not attend church, but instead went to South Carolina with his friend Ms. Shelley and her two daughters. After a long conversation, I found out that Mr. Summers had been sneaking around with Ms. Shelley for years meeting mostly at the town library. Apparently, they had made plans to move in together. Their planned trip to South Carolina was to go in search of a new home. So after listening to the details of the South Carolina trip, I went to the bedroom to call my husband. I asked him about the trip, and of course he denied the story. He accused our daughter of telling lies. I became very angry and told him that his bags would be packed and sitting on the front porch when he got home. Minutes later, he called back and apologized, saying he was only trying to do a friend a favor. He said he drove Ms. Shelley to South Carolina because she did not know how to navigate in the area by herself. He further explained that she was looking to buy a home because her house had caught a fire and had burned to the ground several months ago.

Hours later, my husband came home and was very quiet. He showered and went to sleep on the sofa as usual. The tension became very thick in the home. We completely ignored each other and acted as if we were strangers under the same roof.

Chapter 7
The Move

This was not my husband's first affair, but I had promised myself that it would definitively be the last one I overlooked in our marriage. All the others were swept under the rug, and we went on with our lives as normal once he decided to end the extramarital affair. So why the change with this affair? I'd had enough. I no longer wanted to be in a marriage where this type of behavior was thought to be acceptable and tolerable. I wanted a change for myself and my life.

Several weeks went by, and on this particular Friday, he pretended to go to work. He left around 5:00 a.m. This was later than normal; however, I was scheduled off from work and it was payday. I had many errands to run as well as pay bills. Around 2:00 p.m., I received a call from my husband, who strangely wanted to know my whereabouts. I was hesitant, but I gave little details. I felt something was going on. I asked him if he was going to be home before Jai got off the school bus, and he replied yes.

I arrived home around 4:00 p.m., and my home did not look the same. I walked throughout the house, and I noticed most of his belongings were gone. I walked into my daughter's room, and most of her belongings were gone. I called him on the phone. No answer! I called my daughter. No answer! Around 7:00 p.m., my phone rang and it was him. He told me he was moving far away and was taking our daughter. He threatened to stay in hiding until I signed the divorce papers. He then ended the call.

I called the local police and informed them of the incident. The police officer took the report and assured me that my daughter would be found. An hour later, using the tracking device on my daughter's phone, the officer called me with the whereabouts of my husband and daughter. The officer stated he had talked with my husband, who assured him that he was on a weekend vacation with Jai and that he intended to return to the county on Sunday evening. Hours later, my daughter called and confirmed the story. Jai stated she was in Myrtle Beach with her dad and his girlfriend and would be home on Sunday.

E. Jaroslawa

Chapter 8
God's Move

Late Sunday evening, the doorbell rang. When I opened the door, I noticed Jai standing there alone. Her dad and his girlfriend were leaving the driveway. Jai went to her bedroom and turned on the television. I sat on her bed, and we talked about her time spent with her dad and how much she had missed me. Jai expressed how disappointed she was in her father and wanted to know why things were so different from when we lived in Boston.

I shared how I remembered those ideal days in Boston. We lived a very exciting and happier lifestyle. We were surrounded by fewer people in our circle, but those that around us were very supportive and loving. Maybe life seemed better because we were more dependent on each other and had very few distractions from others. I am not sure. All I knew was that life was very difficult right now.

I looked around and saw that so many life-changing events had occurred and I had not made any steps toward the changes. How could that be? My faith in God had now shown me just how amazing my God is. He can make any change in your life without your help. He can move anyone or anything, no matter the situation or circumstance. In other words, we can be moved without moving. My God! My mother used to say a phrase that her mother used to tell her and others: "God will fix it or remove it in his own way and time."

"Forget the former things; do not dwell
on the past." See, I am doing a new thing!
Now it springs up; do you not perceive
it? I am making a way in the wilderness
and streams in the wasteland.
—Isaiah 43:18–19 (KJV)

My faith was being tested at every angle. I loved and trusted God completely. Still, I was only human and had feelings and emotions running rampant in my head.

One month before the collapse of my marriage, my father passed away at the beloved age of ninety. He was the eldest of eleven siblings and the anchor of the family. He was a veteran of the US Army, where he received a Purple Heart medal for his brave services during Pearl Harbor. He was one of the few survivors of this war tragedy. Days after my father passed, my mom felt a small lump in her breast. Weeks later, she was diagnosed with breast cancer. She was treated with chemotherapy and radiation. Unfortunately, after the treatment, my mom developed dementia, which was brought on by her aggressive treatment.

Life seemed so unfair. I lost my father, part of my mother's true being, and now my marriage. My existence was being challenged. Everything I felt a strong connection to had vanished in a matter of moments. They were what I call my dark moments. Where did I go from there? How did I exist without my father, my mom, or my marriage? Living seemed impossible.

However, I believe what lies before me is destined. These are all ordained moments of my past. I must live through this season, which is required of me to reach my destiny. Uncertainty about my future was controlling my thoughts at that moment. I was facing my greatest fears, which were being without my parents and being a single mom. All my life I feared being without my parents as they were older. My dad was nineteen years older than my mom. My mom was thirty-three and my dad forty-nine when I was conceived. Every day, my dad made me feel so special. He reminded me that I was not a mistake and how much he enjoyed being a father to me at his age. So naturally I became a daddy's girl, just like my four sisters. We loved our dad. He was such a great man. And we loved our mother, who was such a devoted and caring woman. Together, they were an awesome team full of love, support, and wisdom.

The time had come to move on. Life must continue, regardless of my feelings of despair and hurt. It hurt to get out of bed most every morning. The pain of losing everything crushed my spirit. Why is it that hurtful things happen to good people?

Chapter 9
The Changes

The next day, Jai went to school as usual. Life went on as normal without her dad. I decided to change my schedule to accommodate this new life as a single mom. I began to work every Friday, Saturday, and Sunday. This was done so that Jai could spend time with both her parents. Her dad worked Monday through Thursday and was off Friday through Sunday. This plan worked for the challenges that remained in our lives.

More and more, reality seeped in and I began seeing myself as a single mom. I cried every day; therefore, I pushed myself harder every day. I had become my worst critic. Life was very hard, but I managed. I knew I needed to make some changes and adjustments in my life for a brighter future for my daughter, mom, and myself.

So I decided to enroll in classes at a nearby prestigious university. It helped keep my mind busy and avoid thinking about my struggles. Taking classes was a big help. I set a goal for obtaining my degree. I already had some college credits hours; however, I wanted to complete my degree in two years. Each semester I took three or four classes around my work schedule and my days off while helping my sisters care for our elderly mom with dementia.

Two years later, I graduated with my bachelor's degree from the university. This was very rewarding for me. Months later, I enrolled in a masters' program at the same university, where I focused on education, psychology, and counseling. I was very dedicated to my studies and education, and I completed my degree in eighteen months. Shortly after that, I enrolled in a PhD program for health psychology.

Throughout this very challenging period, I had been in and out of court with my husband disputing child custody and divorce issues. Every six to eight weeks I was in court battling him. At every court appearance he managed to create some circus event, even on the days he decided not to appear for whatever reasons. He received great favors in the courtroom, mainly because the county sheriff was his nephew and the clerk of court was his aunt. Even the meddling office assistants working with the clerk were women my husband had slept with during and after our separation. I felt humiliated every time I walked through the court doors. I got rude stares, rude comments, and many eye rolls. I wanted to crumble and die every time I visited the courtroom. I had missed many days from work and exhausted all my vacation time. I spent nearly ten thousand dollars retaining lawyers and paying court fees. I felt I was on trial and so was my family. My husband had smeared our names throughout the muddy waters of the community in which we lived. At times, it felt embarrassing to walk out in public because of the rumors and lies he had manufactured.

E. Jaroslawa

Chapter 10
My Faith

During this time, I have remained faithful with my beliefs, I have accepted myself, and I began to learn how to love myself again, despite my shortcomings. My acceptance of myself came about when I realized that I needed to embrace myself for being who I really was under the surface. I have wants, needs, and desires of my own. I am now free to express those things hidden deep within me because no one else is dominating my life other than God. I am Tia Summers. This is the only person I need to be, and more importantly, the only person I can truly be. I cannot be anyone other than myself. Once this divine intervention took place, I was able to truly love myself for being me.

Looking back, I think about my marriage and

all that it did for me. I was married at the tender age of nineteen. I was in a rush to grow up and be on my own. My parents were totally against me getting married at such an early age. My dad began to accept my decision once he heard from others that I had eloped and was married. He knew it was a bad decision, but he wanted me to be happy. He was my dad and wanted to be in my life regardless of my decision. I believe this was his way of guiding me with his love during the rough journey ahead that could very well have destroyed me. He always reminded me that it was a decision made that we could live through together. He also told me that my husband was not the type of man whom he believed would stay until the end to make it work. My mother, on the other hand, took a while to give her acceptance and blessings. My mom fought against the marriage. She knew I was headed for a great struggle. She later told me that she did not want to see me hurt or go through what she knew was ahead. She felt my husband was truly a man after his own heart and not mine. Several months later, my mom gave in, and our lives went back to normal.

In reviewing my parents' style of loving me, I recognize that sometimes to love something and not be completely consumed by that thing, you need to surrender to it. That was my dad's way of showing his love. However, my mom showed her tenacity and strength by refusing to surrender. Her way of showing love was through resistance and boldness. My mom was unbendable. Her love for Christ and her family made compromising her standards impossible. I learned valuable lessons from both. I love them both. My parents each showed genuine love in their own unique way.

I want so much to live my life to its full potential. I am able to through Christ, who strengthens me. If I keep believing in his words and teachings, I will achieve my goals. I have endured a great measure of loss, and my faith and strength were both challenged; still, I rise each day with hope and forgiveness for all who seek to destroy me.

E. Jaroslawa

Chapter 11

The End

Presently, I can look at my life with such wisdom because I know my steps were ordered by God. This was his perfect plan, not mine. My husband was very unfair and unfaithful to me and our marriage at times. We lived in a marriage for twenty-seven years with lots of lies and pain, causing great hardships that ultimately produced lots of growth. There were some happy days within most of those years. I experienced many feelings and emotions during my marriage. I was married to an overachiever who was obsessed with having things done his way or no way. I can honestly say that I learned a lot from this man. I had a lot of my first experiences with him. He was the first man I made love with. In the beginning we really enjoyed our lovemaking sessions. But soon after the birth of our daughter, everything changed drastically. We were so overwhelmed with being parents that we forgot how to remain friends and lovers. We lost our connection.

Despite the joys, there were many days when I felt suicidal. There were many hours when I drove to and from work that I contemplated ways of ending my life. Strangely, I would spend twelve hours working in a psychiatry unit at a hospital with depressed and suicidal patients. My job description had me prevent patients from doing the very same thing I wanted to do most days. Obviously, my job and marriage were taking a toll on my mind. I became depressed and suicidal. One day I had a conversation with a coworker who was also a friend born and raised in another country. She forever changed my life with a simple advice of words of wisdom. She encouraged me to change my influences and thinking patterns to change my feelings.

Looking back, I now know my husband was placed in my life for a reason, and I believe it was for the season of growth. He was used to push me into my destiny. I believe God gives us what we need, and I needed the push. I needed him to push me into my destiny of becoming the person

I was created to be at a greater summit. What better person to use than someone I felt closest to, someone who knew my weaknesses as well as my strengths? Because of the betrayal by my Judas, I am a much better person. I am a very loving person who cares deeply for my family, friends, and others. Every day, I strive to be the very best I can be without compromising my standards, just as my mom and dad did.

Attending school and going to work were both key ingredients for educating and saving my life. I needed the distraction of keeping my mind busy with positive thoughts and efforts.

E. Jaroslawa

Epilogue
Your Life Matters in the Presence of God

Live your life completely without fear. Set your priorities, prepare adjustments, accept challenges, and perform at your best daily. Life is a precious gift from God. Every day, we should reserve time to experience the presence of God through prayer and worship!

We owe it all to God; he is the creator of our being and universe. Love him today, tomorrow, and forever. Give him thanks and praise! Hallelujah.

God loves us. He is gracious and forgiving. He knows our hearts. He wants us to excel without limits. He is always near us. He has made us a promise that he will never leave nor forsake us. During the darkest moments of my life, especially when I felt so alone, depressed, and at times suicidal, I found these words very comforting. The most valuable lesson gained from my separation and divorce led me to understand why it is so important to be in the presence of God. There you can find many answers to why your life matters.

Forbearing one another, and forgiving one
another, if any man has a quarrel against any:
even as Christ forgave you, so also do ye.
—Colossians 3:13 (KJV)

About the Author

The author is an African American female born and raised in a small, rural community in the United States. She grew up in a large family with loving and supportive parents. As a child, she had a love for books and the sense of serenity it brought to her. Throughout the years, her love for books grew stronger and inspired her to write her very own. Her educational background in psychology and committed work in the health-care field have been amazingly helpful in understanding how important living a fulfilled life without fear is to survival.

The author is a Christian who truly loves the Lord. She believes in his Word and teachings. She aims to be used as a vessel in his works for the good of all people.

Printed in the United States
By Bookmasters